THOSE PASSWORDS BELONG TO

MY WIFI PASSWORDS

LOGIN

User name

Wifi password

                                      OK   CANCEL

LOGIN

User name

Wifi password

                                      OK   CANCEL

LOGIN

User name

Wifi password

                                      OK   CANCEL

MY WIFI PASSWORDS

LOGIN

User name

Wifi password

                        OK   CANCEL

LOGIN

User name

Wifi password

                        OK   CANCEL

LOGIN

User name

Wifi password

                        OK   CANCEL

 www.

IMPORTANT NOT IMPORTANT

⚠️ Verify your information before filling-in to avoid mistakes.

👤 **Username***

🔒 **password***

✉️ **E-mail***

The ones with (*)are very important

📍 **Address**

📞 **Phone number**

Name

Date of birth

❓ **Security questions**

Q :

A :

Q :

A :

Notes

 WWW.

IMPORTANT   NOT IMPORTANT

⚠ Verify your information before filling-in to avoid mistakes.

 Username*

 password*

 E-mail*

The ones with (*) are very important

 Address

 Phone number

 Name

 Date of birth

 **Security questions**

Q :

A :

Q :

A :

Notes

 www.

 IMPORTANT   NOT IMPORTANT

⚠️ Verify your information before filling-in to avoid mistakes.

👤 **Username***

🔓 **password***

✉️ **E-mail***

The ones with (*) are very important

📍 **Address**

📞 **Phone number**

Name

🎂 **Date of birth**

❓ **Security questions**

Q :

A :

Q :

A :

Notes

 www.

IMPORTANT   NOT IMPORTANT

 Verify your information before filling-in to avoid mistakes.

 **Username***

 **password***

✉ **E-mail***

The ones with (*)are very important

📍 **Address**

📞 **Phone number**

Name

Date of birth

❓ **Security questions**

Q :

A :

Q :

A :

Notes

 www.

IMPORTANT   NOT IMPORTANT

⚠ Verify your information before filling-in to avoid mistakes.

Username*

password*

E-mail*

The ones with (*)are very important

Address

Phone number

Name

Date of birth

Security questions

Q :

A :

Q :

A :

Notes

 www.

IMPORTANT   NOT IMPORTANT

⚠️ Verify your information before filling -in to avoid mistakes.

 Username*

 password*

 E-mail*

The ones with (*)are very important

 Address

 Phone number

 Name

 Date of birth

 Security questions

Q :

A :

Q :

A :

Notes

 www.

IMPORTANT NOT IMPORTANT

⚠ Verify your information before filling-in to avoid mistakes.

👤 **Username***

🔓 **password***

✉ **E-mail***

The ones with (*)are very important

📍 **Address**

📞 **Phone number**

Name

🎂 **Date of birth**

❓ **Security questions**

Q :

A :

Q :

A :

Notes

 www.

IMPORTANT   NOT IMPORTANT

⚠ Verify your information before filling-in to avoid mistakes.

 Username*

 password*

 E-mail*

The ones with (*)are very important

 Address

 Phone number

 Name

 Date of birth

 Security questions

Q :

A :

Q :

A :

Notes

 www.

 IMPORTANT   NOT IMPORTANT

⚠ Verify your information before filling-in to avoid mistakes.

👤 **Username***

🔒 **password***

✉ **E-mail***

The ones with (*)are very important

📍 **Address**

📞 **Phone number**

Name

🎂 **Date of birth**

❓ **Security questions**

Q :

A :

Q :

A :

Notes

 www.

IMPORTANT NOT IMPORTANT

⚠ Verify your information before filling-in to avoid mistakes.

 Username*

 password*

 E-mail*

The ones with (*)are very important

 Address

 Phone number

 Name

 Date of birth

 **Security questions**

Q :

A :

Q :

A :

Notes

 www.

IMPORTANT   NOT IMPORTANT

⚠ Verify your information before filling-in to avoid mistakes.

 Username*

🔒 **password***

✉ **E-mail***

The ones with (*)are very important

📍 **Address**

📞 **Phone number**

Name

Date of birth

❓ **Security questions**

Q :

A :

Q :

A :

Notes

 www.

IMPORTANT   NOT IMPORTANT

⚠ Verify your information before filling-in to avoid mistakes.

 Username*

 password*

 E-mail*

The ones with (*)are very important

 Address

 Phone number

 Name

 Date of birth

 Security questions

Q :

A :

Q :

A :

Notes

 www.

IMPORTANT NOT IMPORTANT

⚠ Verify your information before filling-in to avoid mistakes.

📅

Username*

password*

E-mail*

The ones with (*) are very important

Address

Phone number

Name

Date of birth

? Security questions

Q :

A :

Q :

A :

Notes

 WWW.

IMPORTANT   NOT IMPORTANT

⚠ Verify your information before filling-in to avoid mistakes.

 Username*

 password*

 E-mail*

The ones with (*)are very important

 Address

 Phone number

 Name

 Date of birth

 Security questions

Q :

A :

Q :

A :

Notes

 www.

IMPORTANT   NOT IMPORTANT

⚠️ Verify your information before filling-in to avoid mistakes.

 Username*

 password*

 E-mail*

The ones with (*)are very important

 Address

 Phone number

Name

Date of birth

❓ **Security questions**

Q :

A :

Q :

A :

Notes

 www.

IMPORTANT   NOT IMPORTANT

⚠ Verify your information before filling-in to avoid mistakes. 📅

 Username*

 password*

 **E-mail***

The ones with (*) are very important

 **Address**

 **Phone number**

 **Name**

🏛 **Date of birth**

❓ **Security questions**

Q :

A :

Q :

A :

Notes

 www.

IMPORTANT   NOT IMPORTANT

 Verify your information before filling-in to avoid mistakes.

 **Username***

 password*

 E-mail*

The ones with (*) are very important

 Address

 Phone number

 Name

 Date of birth

? **Security questions**

Q :

A :

Q :

A :

Notes

 www.

IMPORTANT   NOT IMPORTANT

⚠️ Verify your information before filling-in to avoid mistakes.

 Username*

 password*

 E-mail*

The ones with (*)are very important

 Address

 Phone number

 Name

 Date of birth

 Security questions

Q :

A :

Q :

A :

Notes

 www.

IMPORTANT  NOT IMPORTANT

⚠️ Verify your information before filling-in to avoid mistakes.

👤 **Username***

🔒 **password***

✉️ **E-mail***

The ones with (*) are very important

📍 **Address**

📞 **Phone number**

🔤 **Name**

🎂 **Date of birth**

❓ **Security questions**

Q :

A :

Q :

A :

Notes

 WWW.

IMPORTANT   NOT IMPORTANT

 Verify your information before filling-in to avoid mistakes.

 Username*

 password*

 E-mail*

The ones with (*) are very important

 Address

 Phone number

 Name

Date of birth

 **Security questions**

Q :

A :

Q :

A :

Notes

🌐 www.

IMPORTANT   NOT IMPORTANT

⚠️ Verify your information before filling-in to avoid mistakes.

📅

👤 **Username***

🔓 **password***

✉️ **E-mail***

The ones with (*)are very important

📍 **Address**

📞 **Phone number**

Name

🎂 **Date of birth**

❓ **Security questions**

Q :

A :

Q :

A :

Notes

 www.

IMPORTANT   NOT IMPORTANT

⚠ Verify your information before filling-in to avoid mistakes.

👤 **Username***

🔒 **password***

✉ **E-mail***

The ones with (*)are very important

📍 **Address**

📞 **Phone number**

 **Name**

 **Date of birth**

        ❓ **Security questions**

Q :

A :

Q :

A :

Notes

 www.

IMPORTANT   NOT IMPORTANT

⚠ Verify your information before filling-in to avoid mistakes.

 **Username***

 **password***

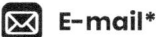 **E-mail***

The ones with (*) are very important

📍 **Address**

📞 **Phone number**

Name

Date of birth

❓ **Security questions**

Q :

A :

Q :

A :

Notes

 www.

IMPORTANT   NOT IMPORTANT

⚠️ Verify your information before filling-in to avoid mistakes.

 Username*

 password*

 E-mail*

The ones with (*)are very important

 Address

 Phone number

 Name

 Date of birth

 **Security questions**

Q :

A :

Q :

A :

Notes

 www.

IMPORTANT   NOT IMPORTANT

⚠ Verify your information before filling-in to avoid mistakes.

Username*

password*

E-mail*

The ones with (*)are very important

Address

Phone number

Name

Date of birth

? Security questions

Q :

A :

Q :

A :

Notes

 WWW.

IMPORTANT   NOT IMPORTANT

⚠ Verify your information before filling-in to avoid mistakes.

 Username*

 password*

 E-mail*

The ones with (*)are very important

 Address

 Phone number

 Name

 Date of birth

 **Security questions**

Q :

A :

Q :

A :

Notes

 www.

IMPORTANT   NOT IMPORTANT

⚠ Verify your information before filling-in to avoid mistakes.

📅

👤 **Username***

🔓 **password***

✉ **E-mail***

The ones with (*)are very important

📍 **Address**

📞 **Phone number**

Name

🎂 **Date of birth**

❓ **Security questions**

Q :

A :

Q :

A :

Notes

 www.

IMPORTANT   NOT IMPORTANT

 Verify your information before filling-in to avoid mistakes.

 Username*

 password*

 E-mail*

The ones with (*)are very important

 **Address**

 Phone number

 Name

 Date of birth

 Security questions

Q :

A :

Q :

A :

Notes

 www.

IMPORTANT   NOT IMPORTANT

⚠️ Verify your information before filling-in to avoid mistakes.

📅

👤 **Username***

🔒 **password***

✉️ **E-mail***

The ones with (*)are very important

📍 **Address**

📞 **Phone number**

📛 **Name**

🏛️ **Date of birth**

❓ **Security questions**

Q :

A :

Q :

A :

Notes

 www.

IMPORTANT   NOT IMPORTANT

 Verify your information before filling-in to avoid mistakes.

 Username*

 password*

 E-mail*

The ones with (*)are very important

 Address

 Phone number

 Name

 **Date of birth**

? **Security questions**

Q :

A :

Q :

A :

Notes

 www.

IMPORTANT   NOT IMPORTANT

⚠️ Verify your information before filling-in to avoid mistakes.

👤 **Username***

🔒 **password***

✉️ **E-mail***

The ones with (*)are very important

📍 **Address**

📞 **Phone number**

Name

🎂 **Date of birth**

❓ **Security questions**

Q :

A :

Q :

A :

Notes

 www.

IMPORTANT   NOT IMPORTANT

 Verify your information before filling-in to avoid mistakes.

 Username*

 password*

✉ **E-mail***

The ones with (*) are very important

📍 **Address**

📞 **Phone number**

Name

Date of birth

❓ **Security questions**

Q :

A :

Q :

A :

Notes

🌐 WWW.

IMPORTANT   NOT IMPORTANT

⚠️ Verify your information before filling-in to avoid mistakes.   📅

👤 **Username***

🔒 **password***

✉️ **E-mail***

The ones with (*)are very important

📍 **Address**

📞 **Phone number**

Name

🎂 **Date of birth**

❓ **Security questions**

Q :

A :

Q :

A :

Notes

 www.

IMPORTANT   NOT IMPORTANT

⚠ Verify your information before filling -in to avoid mistakes.

 Username*

🔓 **password***

✉ **E-mail***

The ones with (*)are very important

📍 **Address**

📞 **Phone number**

 **Name**

 **Date of birth**

❓ **Security questions**

Q :

A :

Q :

A :

Notes

 www.

IMPORTANT   NOT IMPORTANT

⚠ Verify your information before filling-in to avoid mistakes.

 Username*

 password*

 E-mail*

_{The ones with (*) are very important}

 Address

 Phone number

 Name

 Date of birth

 Security questions

Q :

A :

Q :

A :

Notes

 www.

IMPORTANT   NOT IMPORTANT

⚠ Verify your information before filling-in to avoid mistakes.

 Username*

 password*

 E-mail*

The ones with (*) are very important

 Address

 Phone number

 Name

 Date of birth

 **Security questions**

Q :

A :

Q :

A :

Notes

 www.

 IMPORTANT   NOT IMPORTANT

⚠ Verify your information before filling-in to avoid mistakes.

👤 **Username***

🔓 **password***

✉ **E-mail***

The ones with (*) are very important

📍 **Address**

📞 **Phone number**

🏷 **Name**

🎂 **Date of birth**

❓ **Security questions**

Q :

A :

Q :

A :

Notes

 www.

IMPORTANT   NOT IMPORTANT

⚠️ Verify your information before filling-in to avoid mistakes.

 Username*

 password*

 E-mail*

The ones with (*) are very important

 Address

 Phone number

 Name

 Date of birth

 Security questions

Q :

A :

Q :

A :

Notes

 www.

IMPORTANT   NOT IMPORTANT

⚠️ Verify your information before filling-in to avoid mistakes.

👤 **Username***

🔒 **password***

✉️ **E-mail***

The ones with (*) are very important

📍 **Address**

📞 **Phone number**

Name

Date of birth

❓ **Security questions**

Q :

A :

Q :

A :

Notes

 www.

IMPORTANT   NOT IMPORTANT

 Verify your information before filling-in to avoid mistakes.

 Username*

 password*

 E-mail*

The ones with (*) are very important

 **Address**

 **Phone number**

 **Name**

 **Date of birth**

❓ Security questions

Q :

A :

Q :

A :

Notes

 www.

IMPORTANT NOT IMPORTANT

 Verify your information before filling-in to avoid mistakes.

 Username*

 password*

 E-mail*

The ones with (*)are very important

 Address

 Phone number

 Name

 Date of birth

 Security questions

Q :

A :

Q :

A :

Notes

 www.

IMPORTANT   NOT IMPORTANT

 Verify your information before filling -in to avoid mistakes.

 Username*

 password*

 E-mail*

The ones with (*)are very important

 Address

 Phone number

 Name

 Date of birth

 Security questions

Q :

A :

Q :

A :

Notes

 www.

IMPORTANT   NOT IMPORTANT

⚠️ Verify your information before filling-in to avoid mistakes.

👤 **Username***

🔒 **password***

✉️ **E-mail***

The ones with (*)are very important

📍 **Address**

📞 **Phone number**

Name

🎂 **Date of birth**

❓ **Security questions**

Q :

A :

Q :

A :

Notes

 www.

IMPORTANT NOT IMPORTANT

⚠ Verify your information before filling-in to avoid mistakes.

 Username*

🔓 **password***

✉ **E-mail***

The ones with (*) are very important

📍 **Address**

📞 **Phone number**

 Name

🎂 **Date of birth**

 **Security questions**

Q:

A:

Q:

A:

Notes

 www.

IMPORTANT   NOT IMPORTANT

⚠ Verify your information before filling-in to avoid mistakes.

📅

👤 **Username***

🔒 **password***

✉ **E-mail***

The ones with (*)are very important

📍 **Address**

📞 **Phone number**

Name

Date of birth

❓ **Security questions**

Q :

A :

Q :

A :

Notes

 www.

IMPORTANT   NOT IMPORTANT

⚠️ Verify your information before filling-in to avoid mistakes.

- 👤 **Username***
- 🔒 **password***
- ✉️ **E-mail***

The ones with (*) are very important

- 📍 **Address**

- 📞 **Phone number**
- **Name**
- 🎂 **Date of birth**

       ❓ **Security questions**

Q :

A :

Q :

A :

Notes

 WWW.

IMPORTANT   NOT IMPORTANT

⚠ Verify your information before filling-in to avoid mistakes.

 Username*

 password*

 E-mail*

The ones with (*) are very important

 Address

 Phone number

 Name

 Date of birth

 Security questions

Q :

A :

Q :

A :

Notes

 www.

IMPORTANT   NOT IMPORTANT

⚠️ Verify your information before filling-in to avoid mistakes.

 Username*

 password*

 E-mail*

The ones with (*)are very important

 Address

 Phone number

 Name

 Date of birth

 Security questions

Q :

A :

Q :

A :

Notes

 www.

IMPORTANT   NOT IMPORTANT

⚠ Verify your information before filling-in to avoid mistakes.

👤 **Username***

🔓 **password***

✉ **E-mail***

The ones with (*)are very important

📍 **Address**

📞 **Phone number**

Name

Date of birth

❓ **Security questions**

Q :

A :

Q :

A :

Notes

 www.

IMPORTANT   NOT IMPORTANT

 Verify your information before filling-in to avoid mistakes.

 Username*

 password*

✉ **E-mail***

The ones with (*)are very important

 Address

 Phone number

 Name

🎂 **Date of birth**

❓ **Security questions**

Q :

A :

Q :

A :

Notes

 www.

IMPORTANT   NOT IMPORTANT

⚠️ Verify your information before filling-in to avoid mistakes.

👤 **Username***

🔓 **password***

✉️ **E-mail***

The ones with (*)are very important

📍 **Address**

📞 **Phone number**

Name

Date of birth

❓ **Security questions**

Q :

A :

Q :

A :

Notes

 www.

IMPORTANT   NOT IMPORTANT

⚠ Verify your information before filling-in to avoid mistakes.

 Username*

🔒 **password***

✉ **E-mail***

The ones with (*)are very important

📍 **Address**

📞 **Phone number**

 **Name**

 Date of birth

 **Security questions**

Q :

A :

Q :

A :

Notes

 www.

IMPORTANT NOT IMPORTANT

⚠ Verify your information before filling-in to avoid mistakes.

 Username*

 password*

 E-mail*

The ones with (*)are very important

 Address

 Phone number

 Name

 Date of birth

? **Security questions**

Q :

A :

Q :

A :

Notes

 www.

IMPORTANT NOT IMPORTANT

 Verify your information before filling-in to avoid mistakes.

 Username*

 password*

 E-mail*

The ones with (*)are very important

 Address

 Phone number

 Name

 Date of birth

 Security questions

Q :

A :

Q :

A :

Notes

www.

IMPORTANT   NOT IMPORTANT

⚠️ Verify your information before filling-in to avoid mistakes.

Username*

password*

E-mail*

The ones with (*) are very important

Address

Phone number

Name

Date of birth

❓ **Security questions**

Q :

A :

Q :

A :

Notes

 www.

IMPORTANT   NOT IMPORTANT

 Verify your information before filling-in to avoid mistakes.

 Username*

 password*

✉ **E-mail***

The ones with (*) are very important

📍 **Address**

📞 **Phone number**

Name

Date of birth

❓ **Security questions**

Q :

A :

Q :

A :

Notes

 www.

IMPORTANT　　　　NOT IMPORTANT

⚠ Verify your information before filling-in to avoid mistakes.

👤 **Username***

🔒 **password***

✉ **E-mail***

The ones with (*)are very important

📍 **Address**

📞 **Phone number**

Name

🎂 **Date of birth**

❓ **Security questions**

Q :

A :

Q :

A :

Notes

 www.

IMPORTANT   NOT IMPORTANT

⚠ Verify your information before filling -in to avoid mistakes.

 Username*

🔒 **password***

✉ **E-mail***

The ones with (*)are very important

📍 **Address**

📞 **Phone number**

 **Name**

 **Date of birth**

❓ **Security questions**

Q :

A :

Q :

A :

Notes

 www.

IMPORTANT   NOT IMPORTANT

⚠ Verify your information before filling-in to avoid mistakes.

 Username*

 password*

 E-mail*

The ones with (*) are very important

 Address

 Phone number

 Name

 Date of birth

 Security questions

Q :

A :

Q :

A :

Notes

 www.

IMPORTANT   NOT IMPORTANT

 Verify your information before filling-in to avoid mistakes.

 Username*

 password*

 E-mail*

The ones with (*)are very important

 Address

 Phone number

 Name

 Date of birth

 Security questions

Q :

A :

Q :

A :

Notes

 www.

 IMPORTANT   NOT IMPORTANT

⚠ Verify your information before filling-in to avoid mistakes.

👤 **Username***

🔒 **password***

✉ **E-mail***

The ones with (*)are very important

📍 **Address**

📞 **Phone number**

Name

🎂 **Date of birth**

❓ **Security questions**

Q :

A :

Q :

A :

Notes

 www.

IMPORTANT   NOT IMPORTANT

⚠ Verify your information before filling-in to avoid mistakes.

 Username*

 password*

 E-mail*

The ones with (*) are very important

 Address

 Phone number

 Name

 Date of birth

 Security questions

Q :

A :

Q :

A :

Notes

IMPORTANT   NOT IMPORTANT

⚠️ Verify your information before filling-in to avoid mistakes.

👤 **Username***

🔒 **password***

✉️ **E-mail***

The ones with (*) are very important

📍 **Address**

📞 **Phone number**

Name

Date of birth

❓ **Security questions**

Q :

A :

Q :

A :

Notes

 www.

IMPORTANT   NOT IMPORTANT

⚠ Verify your information before filling-in to avoid mistakes.

👤 **Username***

🔒 **password***

✉ **E-mail***

The ones with (*) are very important

📍 **Address**

📞 **Phone number**

Name

Date of birth

❓ **Security questions**

Q :

A :

Q :

A :

Notes

 www.

IMPORTANT   NOT IMPORTANT

⚠ Verify your information before filling-in to avoid mistakes.

 **Username***

 **password***

 **E-mail***

The ones with (*) are very important

👤 **Address**

📞 **Phone number**

Name

Date of birth

❓ **Security questions**

Q:

A:

Q:

A:

Notes

 www.

IMPORTANT   NOT IMPORTANT

⚠ Verify your information before filling-in to avoid mistakes.

 Username*

 password*

 E-mail*

The ones with (*)are very important

 Address

 Phone number

 Name

 Date of birth

 Security questions

Q :

A :

Q :

A :

Notes

 www.

IMPORTANT   NOT IMPORTANT

⚠ Verify your information before filling-in to avoid mistakes.

📅

👤 **Username***

🔒 **password***

✉ **E-mail***

The ones with (*)are very important

📍 **Address**

📞 **Phone number**

🏷 **Name**

🎂 **Date of birth**

        ❓ **Security questions**

Q :

A :

Q :

A :

Notes

 www.

IMPORTANT   NOT IMPORTANT

⚠ Verify your information before filling-in to avoid mistakes.   📅

 Username*

 password*

 E-mail*

The ones with (*)are very important

 Address

 Phone number

 Name

 Date of birth

❓ **Security questions**

Q :

A :

Q :

A :

Notes

 www.

IMPORTANT   NOT IMPORTANT

⚠ Verify your information before filling-in to avoid mistakes.

👤 **Username***

🔒 **password***

✉ **E-mail***

The ones with (*)are very important

📍 **Address**

📞 **Phone number**

Name

🎂 **Date of birth**

❓ **Security questions**

Q :

A :

Q :

A :

Notes

 www.

IMPORTANT　　　NOT IMPORTANT

⚠ Verify your information before filling -in to avoid mistakes.　

 Username*

 password*

 E-mail*

The ones with (*)are very important

 Address

 **Phone number**

 **Name**

 **Date of birth**

 **Security questions**

Q :

A :

Q :

A :

Notes

🌐 www.

IMPORTANT   NOT IMPORTANT

⚠️ Verify your information before filling-in to avoid mistakes.

📅

 **Username***

 **password***

 **E-mail***

The ones with (*) are very important

📍 **Address**

📞 **Phone number**

Name

Date of birth

❓ **Security questions**

Q :

A :

Q :

A :

Notes

 www.

IMPORTANT   NOT IMPORTANT

⚠ Verify your information before filling-in to avoid mistakes.

 Username*

 password*

 E-mail*

The ones with (*)are very important

 Address

 Phone number

 Name

 Date of birth

 **Security questions**

Q :

A :

Q :

A :

Notes

www.

IMPORTANT NOT IMPORTANT

⚠ Verify your information before filling-in to avoid mistakes.

👤 **Username***

🔒 **password***

✉ **E-mail***

The ones with (*)are very important

📍 **Address**

📞 **Phone number**

Name

🎂 **Date of birth**

❓ **Security questions**

Q :

A :

Q :

A :

Notes

 www.

IMPORTANT   NOT IMPORTANT

⚠ Verify your information before filling-in to avoid mistakes.

 Username*

 password*

 E-mail*

The ones with (*) are very important

 Address

 Phone number

 Name

 Date of birth

 **Security questions**

Q :

A :

Q :

A :

Notes

 www.

IMPORTANT NOT IMPORTANT

⚠️ Verify your information before filling-in to avoid mistakes.

👤 **Username***

🔓 **password***

✉️ **E-mail***

The ones with (*)are very important

📍 **Address**

📞 **Phone number**

Name

🎂 **Date of birth**

❓ **Security questions**

Q :

A :

Q :

A :

Notes

 www.

IMPORTANT   NOT IMPORTANT

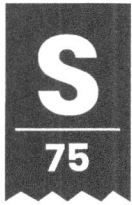

 Verify your information before filling-in to avoid mistakes.

 Username*

 password*

 E-mail*

The ones with (*) are very important

 Address

 Phone number

 Name

 Date of birth

 **Security questions**

Q :

A :

Q :

A :

Notes

WWW.

IMPORTANT   NOT IMPORTANT

 Verify your information before filling-in to avoid mistakes.

 **Username***

 **password***

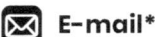 **E-mail***

The ones with (*) are very important

Address

Phone number

Name

Date of birth

Security questions

Q :

A :

Q :

A :

Notes

 WWW.

IMPORTANT   NOT IMPORTANT

⚠️ Verify your information before filling-in to avoid mistakes.

 Username*

 password*

 E-mail*

The ones with (*)are very important

 Address

 Phone number

 Name

 Date of birth

 **Security questions**

Q :

A :

Q :

A :

Notes

 www.

IMPORTANT   NOT IMPORTANT

⚠ Verify your information before filling-in to avoid mistakes.

👤 **Username***

🔒 **password***

✉ **E-mail***

The ones with (*)are very important

📍 **Address**

📞 **Phone number**

Name

🎂 **Date of birth**

❓ **Security questions**

Q :

A :

Q :

A :

Notes

 WWW.

IMPORTANT   NOT IMPORTANT

 Verify your information before filling-in to avoid mistakes.

 **Username***

 **password***

✉ **E-mail***

The ones with (*) are very important

📍 **Address**

📞 **Phone number**

Name

Date of birth

❓ **Security questions**

Q :

A :

Q :

A :

Notes

 WWW.

IMPORTANT NOT IMPORTANT

 Verify your information before filling-in to avoid mistakes.

Username*

password*

E-mail*

The ones with (*) are very important

Address

Phone number

Name

Date of birth

Security questions

Q :

A :

Q :

A :

Notes

 www.

IMPORTANT   NOT IMPORTANT

⚠️ Verify your information before filling-in to avoid mistakes.   📅

 Username*

🔓 **password***

✉️ **E-mail***

The ones with (*) are very important

📍 **Address**

📞 **Phone number**

 **Name**

 **Date of birth**

 **Security questions**

Q :

A :

Q :

A :

Notes

🌐 WWW.

IMPORTANT   NOT IMPORTANT

⚠️ Verify your information before filling-in to avoid mistakes.   📅

👤 **Username***

🔒 **password***

✉️ **E-mail***

The ones with (*) are very important

📍 **Address**

📞 **Phone number**

Name

Date of birth

❓ **Security questions**

Q :

A :

Q :

A :

Notes

 www.

IMPORTANT NOT IMPORTANT

⚠ Verify your information before filling-in to avoid mistakes.

 Username*

 password*

 E-mail*

The ones with (*) are very important

 Address

 Phone number

 Name

 Date of birth

 Security questions

Q :

A :

Q :

A :

Notes

 WWW.

IMPORTANT   NOT IMPORTANT

⚠️ Verify your information before filling-in to avoid mistakes.

👤 **Username***

🔓 **password***

✉️ **E-mail***

The ones with (*) are very important

📍 **Address**

📞 **Phone number**

Name

🎂 **Date of birth**

❓ **Security questions**

Q :

A :

Q :

A :

Notes

 WWW.

IMPORTANT   NOT IMPORTANT

 Verify your information before filling-in to avoid mistakes.

 Username*

 password*

 E-mail*

The ones with (*)are very important

 Address

 Phone number

 Name

 Date of birth

        ? Security questions

Q :

A :

Q :

A :

Notes

 WWW.

IMPORTANT NOT IMPORTANT

 Verify your information before filling-in to avoid mistakes.

 **Username***

 password*

 E-mail*

The ones with (*)are very important

 Address

 Phone number

 Name

 Date of birth

? **Security questions**

Q :

A :

Q :

A :

Notes

 www.

IMPORTANT   NOT IMPORTANT

 Verify your information before filling-in to avoid mistakes.

 Username*0

 password*0

 E-mail*0

The ones with (*)are very important

 Address

 Phone number

 Name

 Date of birth

        ? **Security questions**

Q :

A :

Q :

A :

Notes

 www.

IMPORTANT   NOT IMPORTANT

 Verify your information before filling-in to avoid mistakes.

 **Username***

 **password***

 **E-mail***

The ones with (*) are very important

Address

Phone number

Name

Date of birth

Security questions

Q :

A :

Q :

A :

Notes

 WWW.

IMPORTANT   NOT IMPORTANT

⚠ Verify your information before filling-in to avoid mistakes.

 Username*

 password*

 E-mail*

The ones with (*)are very important

 Address

 Phone number

 Name

 Date of birth

 **Security questions**

Q :

A :

Q :

A :

Notes

 www.

IMPORTANT　　　　　NOT IMPORTANT

⚠ Verify your information before filling-in to avoid mistakes.

 **Username***

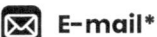 **password***

✉ **E-mail***

The ones with (*) are very important

📍 **Address**

📞 **Phone number**

Name

🎂 **Date of birth**

❓ **Security questions**

Q :

A :

Q :

A :

Notes

www.

IMPORTANT   NOT IMPORTANT

⚠ Verify your information before filling -in to avoid mistakes.

 **Username***

 **password***

✉ **E-mail***

The ones with (*)are very important

📍 **Address**

📞 **Phone number**

🏷 **Name**

🎂 **Date of birth**

❓ **Security questions**

Q :

A :

Q :

A :

Notes

🌐 WWW.

IMPORTANT   NOT IMPORTANT

⚠️ Verify your information before filling-in to avoid mistakes.

📅

👤 **Username***

🔓 **password***

✉️ **E-mail***

The ones with (*)are very important

📍 **Address**

📞 **Phone number**

🏷️ **Name**

🎂 **Date of birth**

❓ **Security questions**

Q :

A :

Q :

A :

Notes

 www.

IMPORTANT   NOT IMPORTANT

 Verify your information before filling-in to avoid mistakes.

 **Username***

 **password***

 **E-mail***

The ones with (*) are very important

🗺️ **Address**

📞 **Phone number**

Name

Date of birth

❓ **Security questions**

Q :

A :

Q :

A :

Notes

IMPORTANT   NOT IMPORTANT

 Verify your information before filling-in to avoid mistakes.

 **Username***

 password*

✉ **E-mail***

The ones with (*)are very important

📍 **Address**

📞 **Phone number**

Name

Date of birth

❓ **Security questions**

Q :

A :

Q :

A :

Notes

 WWW.

IMPORTANT NOT IMPORTANT

 96

 Verify your information before filling-in to avoid mistakes.

 Username*

 password*

 E-mail*

The ones with (*)are very important

 Address

 Phone number

 Name

 Date of birth

 Security questions

Q :

A :

Q :

A :

Notes

 www.

 IMPORTANT   NOT IMPORTANT

⚠️ Verify your information before filling-in to avoid mistakes.

👤 **Username***

🔓 **password***

✉️ **E-mail***

The ones with (*)are very important

📍 **Address**

📞 **Phone number**

🏷️ **Name**

🎂 **Date of birth**

❓ **Security questions**

Q :

A :

Q :

A :

Notes

 WWW.

IMPORTANT   NOT IMPORTANT

⚠ Verify your information before filling-in to avoid mistakes.

 Username*

 password*

 E-mail*

The ones with (*) are very important

 Address

 Phone number

 Name

 Date of birth

 Security questions

Q :

A :

Q :

A :

Notes

 www.

IMPORTANT   NOT IMPORTANT

⚠ Verify your information before filling-in to avoid mistakes.

👤 **Username***

🔓 **password***

✉ **E-mail***

The ones with (*)are very important

📍 **Address**

📞 **Phone number**

Name

🎂 **Date of birth**

❓ **Security questions**

Q :

A :

Q :

A :

Notes

 www.

IMPORTANT　　　NOT IMPORTANT

⚠ Verify your information before filling-in to avoid mistakes.

 Username*

 password*

 E-mail*

The ones with (*) are very important

 Address

 Phone number

 Name

 Date of birth

 Security questions

Q :

A :

Q :

A :

Notes

 WWW.

IMPORTANT   NOT IMPORTANT

⚠ Verify your information before filling-in to avoid mistakes.

 Username*

🔒 **password***

✉ **E-mail***

The ones with (*)are very important

📍 **Address**

📞 **Phone number**

🏷 **Name**

🎂 **Date of birth**

❓ **Security questions**

Q :

A :

Q :

A :

Notes

 WWW.

IMPORTANT   NOT IMPORTANT

⚠ Verify your information before filling-in to avoid mistakes.

 Username*

 password*

 E-mail*

The ones with (*)are very important

 Address

 Phone number

 Name

 Date of birth

 **Security questions**

Q :

A :

Q :

A :

Notes

 WWW.

IMPORTANT NOT IMPORTANT

⚠ Verify your information before filling-in to avoid mistakes.

👤 **Username***

🔓 **password***

✉ **E-mail***

The ones with (*)are very important

📍 **Address**

📞 **Phone number**

Name

🎂 **Date of birth**

❓ **Security questions**

Q :

A :

Q :

A :

Notes

 www.

IMPORTANT   NOT IMPORTANT

 Verify your information before filling-in to avoid mistakes.

 Username*

 password*

 E-mail*

The ones with (*) are very important

 Address

 Phone number

 Name

Date of birth

Security questions

Q :

A :

Q :

A :

Notes

Error!

 There is not enough pages, time to buy a new book !

www.ingramcontent.com/pod-product-compliance
Lightning Source LLC
Chambersburg PA
CBHW070421220526
45466CB00004B/1496